EASTER

Program Builder

No. 23

Resources for the Creative Easter Program Planner

Compiled by

Paul M. Miller and Scott Stargel

Lillenas Publishing Co.
Kansas City, MO 64141

lillenas.com

New Life

Easter is one of those seasons we cherish. It is a season of hope and color, of fun and faith. It is a season when families come together to celebrate.

And Easter is more. It is a time of new life. New life: a chick is hatched from an egg. New life: flowers appear to shake off the chill of winter. New life. This collection of recitations, exercises, and sketches focuses on that new life.

The special person of Jesus—His life, suffering, death, and resurrection—gives us new life. Use this collection to put together your special Easter or Lenten program. There are recitations for the smaller ones and monologues and sketches for the older ones. Use them to supplement your service, or be creative in combining them into a full-length program.

Here at Lillenas, we pray that your Easter program will be specially blessed and filled with the new life of Christ.

—Scott Stargel

Easter Joy

Easter is a time of joy,
For every girl and boy.

—Anthony Lamson

Even Me

Jesus died for me.
Yes! Even little me.

Jesus rose again for me
Yes! Even little me.

Jesus loves all of us,
Yes! Even little me.

—Linda M. Basler

Little Bee

(For a little one dressed as a bee)

I'm a little bee,
Made by God,
For all to see.
Happy Easter!

—Anthony Lamson

Jesus Is Alive! Hallelujah!

May God reign supreme in your life.
Not just this Easter Day,
But all year through!

—Evangeline Carey

Easter Flowers

(A little one carries Easter lilies. Have other children ready to hand out to pastor, guests, etc.)

See the flowers,
One, two, three.
They're for Easter.
For Jesus, you see.

—Anthony Lamson

Such Love

Would Christ have been so kind,
To die to save just me?
How much love He must have had,
Such love, such love for me?

—Linda M. Basler

God Bless Your Easter

Jesus loved us enough
To die and rise again.
May you feel that love today,
And may it bless your Easter
In a very special way!

—Evangeline Carey

He Is Alive! Hallelujah!

May you grasp the good news of
Easter
In all of its beauty,
As you celebrate what Jesus
Did for you and me,
When He died on Calvary.

—Evangeline Carey

Have a Very Happy Easter

May you share in the celebration
Of the Risen Jesus Christ,
And may your heart rejoice
During this blessed Easter!

—Evangeline Carey

Jesus' Day

Hunting eggs sure is fun,
And bunnies sure are soft.
But Easter is more than those
It's Jesus' day. All right!

—Linda M. Basler

Christ Is the Source

Christ is the source of Easter,
Because He lives.
And, He is God.
May He be your source today
And reign within your heart!

—Evangeline Carey

Power Acrostic

(Have speakers hold up letters as they say their line. Then on final word, flip over cards to spell "ALIVE."

P is for the Palms they waved when Jesus entered town.

O is for the Offerings of praise they gave Him.

W is for the Women who gathered at His cross.

E is for the Early morning at the tomb.

R is for the Resurrection, when Christ arose.

God's power gives us Easter,
because Jesus is alive!

—Linda M. Basler

Christ Is Risen

Easter's coming! Easter's coming!
Sing a joyful song.
Let the birds join in the chorus.
Sing it all day long.

Christ is risen! Christ is risen!
That is why we sing.
Jesus died and rose to save us.
Now He is our King.

—Margaret Primrose

Two Crowns

They spit on Him.
They whipped His back.
They tweaked His beard,
And laughed!
They crowned His head
With cruel thorns,
And led Him forth
To die!

But He rose again!
And the day will come
When at His feet
They all will bow
And beg for mercy
With trembling lips.

No more will He
Endure their scorn,
For on His head will rest
A crown of gold,
And He'll ride forth
In power and might,
Forever more
to reign!

Have a Wonderful Easter!

Jesus is truly alive!
May you feel it in your heart today,
And may the news
Bless you in a very special way!

—Evangeline Carey

New Creatures

(Children should be dressed in appropriate outfits: antenna for CATERPILLAR, *white blanket for* COCOON, *wings for* BUTTERFLY, *ragged-dirty shirt over nice clean clothes for* NEW CHRISTIAN.*)*

CATERPILLAR:

I'm just a tiny caterpillar,
An old green worm to you.
I crawl around on the ground all day
And wash my face in the dew.
I eat and eat my greens every day,
I'm very plain in every single way.

COCOON:

Once a caterpillar, that I was.
Now just wrapped in a soft down fuzz,
I'll sleep for weeks and have no clue
Of how I'll change into something new.

BUTTERFLY:

Look at me! Can you believe your eyes?
I slept in a cocoon and woke to this surprise!
I'm a different creature! I've been made new,
Just like the wonderful change
That can happen to you.

NEW CHRISTIAN:

My life was filled with sorrow and sin.
I was dirty old rags till I asked Jesus in.
(Removes shirt) He took my life and turned me about,
I'm clean! Forgiven! Hear me shout!

ALL:

Jesus died, was buried, and then,
Left the grave and rose again.
His blood He shed for you and me,
So believe in Him. He'll set you free!

—*Sharon Kaye Kiesel*

My Jesus—My King

My Jesus who died
was crucified
on a bare wooden cross so old.

After He died
He was placed inside
a tomb so lonely and cold.

On the third day
the stone rolled away
opening wide the door.

Angels stood near
who said, "He's not here,
Jesus now lives evermore."

My King paid the price.
He didn't think twice.
That's how much He loves you and me.

He gave up His life,
suffered pain and strife,
to redeem us and set us free.

Someday over crowds
we'll see in the clouds
as Jesus returns in love.

Believers He'll call.
We'll come one and all
to join Him in heaven above.

—*Sharon Kaye Kiesel*

Jesus, King and Savior

An Exercise for Children and Choir

By Grace Richie

Setting:

The table is placed center stage. The urns are scattered around the stage to hold the palm branches decoratively.

Props:

Table, urns, palm branches, donkey (or image), bread, goblet, basin, towel, crown of thorns, cross, lily, and golden crown.

(Choir sings a Hosanna chorus or similar hymn as children enter waving palm branches. Several adults are included to give impression of families. Upon reaching the front, the children place the palm branches in the urns and then take their seats on the first row.)

NARRATOR: Palm Sunday was so named because the people that followed Jesus had taken branches from the low palm bushes along the highway into Jerusalem, and as they waved them they sang, "Hosanna! Blessed is he who comes in the name of the Lord, even the King of Israel." John says that the branches of palm trees were used in this way as tokens of victory and peace . . . an appropriate symbol for the King of Kings and Prince of Peace.

Jesus did not *walk* that day, as He usually did. Instead, He rode on a donkey. Most kings rode strong, beautiful horses. Why did Jesus, the Savior King, ride a donkey? It is recorded that the kings of Israel rode on donkeys to show humility and lowliness. (CHILD *brings in image of donkey and places it in appropriate spot.)* It was also predicted in Zechariah 9:9 that the Messiah would enter Jerusalem "humble and riding on a donkey."

(CHOIR *sings first and second verses of "Ride on, Ride on in Majesty" or similar song.)*

NARRATOR: During the next few days Jesus cleansed the Temple, told parables about the kingdom of God, and had His authority questioned. Also, it was during this time that one of His disciples, Judas, made plans to betray his Lord. On Thursday of that week, Jesus and the 12 disciples celebrated the annual Feast of the Passover together in the upper room of a friend's house. As they sat around the table. (CHILD *brings in large loaf of bread and places it on table.)* Jesus took the bread and said, "Whenever you eat bread remember my body that is broken for you." (CHILD *brings in large goblet and places it next to the bread.)* Then Jesus took a cup of wine and said, "This is my blood shed for the forgiveness of sins." These words of Jesus made the disciples uneasy because they did not fully understand what He meant at that time.

(CHOIR *sings two or three verses from a Communion hymn.)*

NARRATOR: Supper was over. Judas had left. Now Jesus taught the disciples a very important lesson. It was the custom in those days for servants to wash the feet of guests who came into the home, but, since no servant was present at this supper, no dusty feet had been washed. (CHILD *brings in a basin, placing it in front of the table.)* So, Jesus took a basin. He filled it with water (CHILD *brings in a towel and places it on the edge of the basin),* and He took a towel and began to wash and dry the disciples' feet. Peter objected, but Jesus said, "If I do not wash you, you have no part in me."

When Jesus had finished washing the disciples' feet, He said, "You call me Master and Lord, and that is true. Since I, the Lord and Teacher, have washed your feet, you ought to wash one another's feet. A servant is not greater than his master, nor the master greater than the servant."

The basin and the towel, therefore, are symbols of servanthood.

After all of this, Jesus and His disciples went to the Garden of Gethsemane where Jesus went apart from them to pray.

(CHOIR *sings "Go to Dark Gethsemane" or similar.)*

NARRATOR: Later that night, as Jesus came to wake His sleeping disciples, soldiers . . . led by Judas . . . came and arrested Him. He was taken before the high priest and accused of blasphemy; then to Pilate, the governor. False witnesses testified against Jesus. (CHILD *brings in crown of thorns and places it in an appropriate spot.)* He was beaten and mocked and the soldiers made a crown of thorns and pressed it on His head until the blood ran down over His face. When Pilate brought Jesus before the crowd, he wanted to release Him, but the crowd shouted, "Crucify him! Crucify him!" Pilate gave in to their demands, and Jesus was led away to Golgotha to be crucified. (CHILD *brings in table cross and places it on the table behind the loaf and goblet. If a large cross is available, it can be positioned behind the table.)*

Both the crown of thorns and the Cross were symbols of shame and guilt. Thorns, in particular, throughout biblical history were symbolic of sin. So it was that Jesus, the perfect One, who took the shame and guilt of sin for you and me.

(CHOIR *sings "Were You There?" or similar.)*

NARRATOR: Jesus *died* on that cross, but that was not the end of the story. Three days later God raised Him from that death. He was seen alive by the believers. (CHILD *brings in lilies and places them on table.)* Not only is the lily a symbol of purity and truth, but it represents hope and joy in the Easter promise of eternal life as well.

(CHILD *brings in golden crown and places it over the cross.)* And, instead of a crown of thorns, the golden crown of victory belongs to Jesus. Remember what the angel said to the women at the tomb? "Do not seek the living among the dead. He is not here . . . He is risen!"

(CHOIR *sings "Now Is Christ Risen from the Dead" or similar stirring hymn about the Resurrection.)*

Look Down from the Cross

A Monologue

by Marjorie Stump

When I was brave and very young, I promised to follow Christ. Obediently, I made plans to suffer and sacrifice in the service of our Savior.

"Yes, Lord," I announced, "I will bear my cross and follow You."

Together we climbed that long hill. The road was bumpy and steep. A rude crowd followed and laughed. Friends turned away. Loved ones criticized. Finally, on the crest of the hill, the executioner waited, and the act was accomplished with skill and surprising speed. After the first moments of agonizing pain, after the numbness, I looked down to view the world from a new perspective.

I could see the whole world as Christ saw it. I watched the people—but I did not love them. I wanted to leap down and strike out in revenge against a thoughtless, sinful multitude. Even from the cross, Christ's point of view had not yet become my own point of view.

Remembering His words, I could almost hear His voice saying, "Father, forgive them; for they know not what they do."

I tried to speak. "Father," I called. But the forgiveness caught in my throat. I was not divine—and I did not want to forgive.

Angrily, I complained: "Look over there. That dishonest politician has taken a bribe. Those men are selling drugs. That mother has abused and abandoned her children. Those boys have robbed and killed."

I saw wars and wantonness, death and devastation. I watched it all from the cross, and I did not like what I saw. I wanted to be free. Those sinners did not know that I was up there on that cross. I was suffering, and they did not appreciate it.

"Lord," I cried, "get me down from here!"

"No," Christ answered. "Not yet. It is not finished."

"How long does it take?" I asked.

"That is up to you," He said.

"I am ready now!" I replied.

"No," He said, "you are not ready. Your selfishness is growing instead of dying."

"But, Lord," I argued, "it did not take You this long to die."

"That is true," Jesus answered. "I went to the Cross because I love those people out there."

Several moments passed before He asked, "Why did you come to the cross?"

Behind a camouflage of false confidence, I hurried to explain. "We were taught that each Christian must take up his or her cross and follow You—and so I did. I wanted to be sure of my place in the Kingdom."

"You wanted to be sure." He spoke the words sadly. "You wanted to receive. Faith in Me is a giving faith. You did not come to the cross to give your life for others; you are seeking a reward for yourself."

"No! No!" I tried to defend myself. "I wanted to do the *right* thing. I want to do something *important* for You. I want to be a *good* Christian!"

"Ambition!" He spoke sharply, and His quiet voice brought tears to my eyes.

I could no longer meet His eyes, but I could hear Him saying, "Assurance! Reward! Ambition! Whatever happened to faith, peace, and love?"

"I don't know, Lord," I admitted. A feeling of guilt engulfed my whole being, bringing my heart to repentance.

"Father God," I whispered, "please forgive me."

I waited an incredibly long time. It seemed to be hours, days, even years. I felt a dull, burning ache—an ache that gradually eased and finally passed away. Selfishness was dying. Slowly. Painfully.

Again, I looked down from the cross.

The world appeared to be exactly as I had seen it before, but *I* had changed. I watched the same persons—yet now, in their acts of hatred and violence, I was able to recognize my own feelings and failures. I saw the temptations and sins of others with compassion and forgiveness. I was beginning to experience God's love living through me. I wanted to help those people out there—not for ambition, nor for reward, but for the benefit of those persons who need to know God's love.

Then, suddenly, in one final moment, the cross was gone.

It was as if I had been crucified with Christ. My death had not accomplished salvation for anyone. Only God's Son could do away with the sins of the world. My selfishness was buried, and I rose now to walk the new life with Christ. I stood free, ready to go down and serve among the people.

We moved slowly down that mountain while somewhere in the distance a choir chanted softly "Not by might, nor by power, but by my Spirit, says the Lord of hosts."

Amen.

In the Land

A Monologue

by Margaret Primrose

(SIMON, *a pilgrim from Cyrene, enters.)*

Four hundred miles I traveled from Cyrene to Jerusalem for Passover. The journey was my lifelong dream—the dream of every Jew who lives abroad—but an unexplainable urgency prompted me to make the trip from my African port city that year.

After long, empty days of watching the oarsmen ply the Mediterranean in monotonous rhythm, we docked near Jerusalem. I hurried to the Holy City and began my search for family I had never met. Together we would eat the Passover lamb, and together we would gaze at the majestic Temple.

The Pool of Siloam, the palace of the high priests—so often I had heard of them from my father that they seemed almost familiar. After many queries, I found my uncle, Jacob, who welcomed me into his home.

He was eager to introduce me to everyone as his nephew, Simon of Cyrene, to all who came into his house, but nobody would talk of anything except a Man called Jesus. Some people ranted, gestured, and labeled him an imposter who dared to call himself King of the Jews. Others were convinced that He was, indeed, the long-awaited Messiah.

I? I listened in confused and deepening disappointment. I had hoped for some guided tours of the area, not speculation about the latest zealot who hoped to overthrow the Romans.

The Temple seemed little more than a marketplace and slaughterhouse for sacrificial lambs. Was there no way to appreciate its grandeur without distancing myself from it? Where was the peace I should have found there?

Plodding along that awesome Friday, I wandered into a Golgotha-bound mob. Three condemned men there were, and each of them was struggling under the weight of a cross. One looked especially weak and pallid, but there was an unusual serenity about Him even as the crowd shouted, "Crucify Him! Away with Him!"

I gasped as He stumbled and fell. The Roman soldiers were impatient, eager to be done with their inglorious task.

"That one!" The Roman in charge pointed to me. Immediately, one of the burliest soldiers seized me, and a pair of them heaved the despicable cross on my back. Still another slanted a sword at me and ordered me to carry the cross.

Anger exploded inside me, but I dared not protest. I, who felt I had done nothing to deserve it, was treated like a criminal, a sinner!

I hated the man and hated the Romans. Let them spear Him to death if He was too weak to carry His own cross, I thought.

Intense pain etched the face of the condemned, but He uttered no complaint. His eyes spoke gently to me, but I sensed that He did not expect me to understand. Then He calmly led the climb up Golgotha. Fire raged within me as I followed.

At the crest of the hill I was freed. Panting and waving my fists, I ran from the scene. I heard the man's name, Jesus, but He was nothing to me. The bizarre stories of His miracles were not true. A Messiah would not walk calmly to his death.

I raved about the way the Romans treated me. I fumed when I heard that the Man's followers had scattered. Where was the brash and bold Peter, the one reported to brag that he would die for his Master?

On the third day there were more strange tales. Jesus had died—I did not doubt that—but, supposedly, He was alive again. Was that true, or had His disciples risked their lives to steal His body? An entire band of guards were assigned to watch His grave. Would all of them fall asleep knowing that they could be put to death for not guarding the tomb properly?

I pondered it and put off my return to Cyrene. I hoped and feared to encounter Jesus or His disciples. It was said that He had ascended into the clouds but would return. At last I determined to seek out His followers.

Peter had stopped bragging before I met him, but he was a bold one. "Jesus' cross," he said, "was really mine. Jesus died for *my* sins. Mine!"

Now I understood the Cross, but what a painful revelation it was! I had a choice to accept or reject Jesus. I chose Jesus. I became a follower of Jesus.

Peter became my mentor. How fearless he was in telling even rioters to repent of their sins. Someday Peter will die for that, but that's OK. Peter chose the cross before anyone could choose his death.

I was not ready for that. In effect, I was running from cross-bearing. At least I could forgive Peter because he once ran from the cross. How could he choose it now?

Today I found out, and I will never be the same because of it. Today, they crucified Peter. But, Peter was not the first to take a cross. His master was.

Nor did Jesus follow me that day we climbed Golgotha. *He* was in the lead. He is *always* in the lead. Always!

The Temp

A Monologue

by Becky Garrison

Setting:
Jerusalem Office Services building. At center is a desk with a chair and telephone. The desk is cluttered with files and papers.

Props:
Desk, chair, telephone, miscellaneous desk supplies, file folders, and paper.

(Lights come up on MISS WHIPPET *at her desk, sorting through the various mounds of papers. The telephone rings, and she immediately answers it.)*

Jerusalem Office Services, may I help You? . . . We provide top-notch quality temporary workers for every type of job situation, so I'm sure I can be of assistance. Your name please? . . . Mr. God . . . Oh, You want to be called just God. That's OK; we can be a little informal if need be. Anything to please the customer. You can call me Marjorie or Miss Whippet, whichever You prefer. Now I need Your mailing address? . . . Thy Kingdom Come, c/o The Heavens and the Earth. Are You sure You'll get Your bill if I send it there? . . . If You say so.

Now, how can I help You? . . . uh, huh . . . Well, I wouldn't call Your request for a Messiah unusual. Why don't You tell me what You're looking for, and I'll see what I can do . . . Good public speaking and people skills. No problem. We have customer service representatives, hostesses, and product demonstrators . . . I'll have to place a call over to our industrial division to see if they have any carpenters available

(Embarrassed) I'm sorry, God, but I don't know if my clients were born of virgins. Federal law prohibits me from asking highly personal questions, You know. Any other requests? . . . Well, we do have a medical division, but You know, it's going to be hard to find someone with carpentry *and* healing skills. But, let me try and see what I can do.

Anything else? . . . No one can change water into wine, but I can get You someone who was a former bartender. You know, I hate to be discouraging, God, but this job is starting to get a little hard to fill . . . Well, I wouldn't say our temps are perfect, but we do screen them very carefully. Hmm, You want perfect, though? Well, I'll see.

Miracles? You want someone to perform miracles. I have a woman who can type 90 words per minute, has excellent dictaphone and shorthand, is raising three children as a single parent, volunteers as a Cub Scout den mother, and can bake a mean souffle. I think that's a miracle if I ever saw one.

You want someone to suffer upon a cross for the sins of humankind? I ask a lot of our temps, but that's pushing it. You know, God, we'll have to charge a fair amount for an assignment like this.

Are You serious? I can't ask my workers to pay with their lives for an assignment. I don't care how good it is . . .

And they have to what? You mean actually *rise* from the dead. Are You out of your mind? Sorry, God, I can't fill that job. I don't think anyone can.

Good day. *(She hangs up the phone as lights go out.)*

Raised with the King

by Jamie J. Puckett and Kerry S. Knight

Cast:

JAMES, *the brother of Jesus*
ANNA, *the sister of Jesus*
NARRATOR, *can also be read by* JAMES *or* ANNA *(as indicated) out of character*

Setting:

Bare stage. JAMES and ANNA are young children in Scene 1. In Scenes 2 and 3 they are adults.

Props:

All props are pantomimed

Scene 1

(Stage is dark. NARRATOR *speaks as lights come up.)*

NARRATOR (ANNA): The Bible tells us that Jesus, the Son of God, was born long ago in Bethlehem to a young couple named Mary and Joseph. Jesus was the spotless lamb that was to become the Sacrifice for all of our sins. He was perfect. He was tempted in all things as we are, yet without sin. He committed no sin and in Him there was no sin. Jesus Christ, the perfect Son of God, was raised in the city of Nazareth along with His brothers and sisters. But, what did *they* think about this very special sibling among them? Have you ever wondered what it would be like to grow up with a perfect brother? [Hebrews 4:15, 1 Peter 2:22]

NARRATOR (JAMES): Remember, a prophet is never accepted in his own home.

(ANNA *runs in and gets* JAMES's *attention for a game of hopscotch.)*

ANNA: Come on, James. Get your rock. Let's play!

JAMES: OK! *(Searching)* Where did I leave that thing? Oh, here it is. Let's go!

ANNA: It's my turn first. *(She throws her rock and jumps a few step as if playing hopscotch.* JAMES *then throws his rock and begins to jump.* ANNA *looks up as if her mother, Mary, has entered.)* Oh, hi, Mom. Hey, where are you going? To the market?

JAMES *(stopping in midjump, asks resentfully):* Are you going to take Jesus with you?

ANNA: Well, of course she is, James. She always takes Jesus to the market because He helps her carry her bags.

JAMES: But, I like to push the cart.

ANNA: Yeah, but you always run over the back of her ankles.

JAMES *(defensive):* It's an accident! Heaven forbid that Jesus should do anything wrong.

ANNA: Well, if He ever runs over her feet, at least He apologizes afterward.

JAMES: I guess that's true. *(Whining)* But still, He always gets to go everywhere.

ANNA: Oh, don't be such a baby. He'll probably just run off somewhere like He did last time, and we'll have to go look for Him.

JAMES: As if I don't have anything more important to do than wander all over Jerusalem looking for my brother. *(He goes back to his "important" game of hopscotch.)* OK, I'm going for the whole thing this time. *(He takes a few jumps, but then messes up and quits.)* I'm not good at this game!

ANNA: Wow, Jesus can always get all the way there and back in one shot.

JAMES *(sarcastically):* Oh, I'll bet He can, the little mister Hopscotch-King-of-the-Jews.

ANNA: Look, James, I know He's a little annoying sometimes, but you have to admit, He's a good guy.

JAMES: Good! He's perfect! He always gets to help Dad at work because He works *so* hard and does *such* a good job. And if Dad ever gets thirsty while He's working, there goes Jesus off to the well to bring him some water. Sometimes, I wish He'd just fall in that well and stay there for a month. *(They start to laugh, but quit, obviously surprised that Mary is still listening.)*

BOTH: We're sorry, Mom.

JAMES: But it's just that He . . .

ANNA: Be quiet, James. Here He comes.

BOTH: Hi, Jesus.

(JAMES *whispers a devious plan to* ANNA *and they laugh secretively.)*

JAMES *(pointing up into the distance):* Hey, Jesus, look over there. A star shining bright in the sky.

(ANNA *"pushes" Jesus then hurries back to her brother as they both giggle. They stop giggling at the same time as if they've been caught.)*

ANNA: What? *(Defensive)* I didn't touch You. I didn't touch You. How could You possibly know which one of us touched You? You were facing the other way! *(She looks up to her mom.)* Mom, I didn't touch Him. He's lying.

JAMES *(amused):* Now, Anna, Mom knows better than that.

ANNA *(gives* JAMES *a dirty look and then faces Mary):* Yes, ma'am. I'm sorry, Jesus.

JAMES: Oh, are you guys leaving already? Well, have fun at the market. Oh and Jesus, could You bring me back some water? Or, maybe you'd better make it wine. *(They laugh and give each other high-fives.)*

BOTH *(innocently turning to Jesus):* Just kidding.

ANNA: Bye, Mom. Bye, Jesus. See you later! Wait . . . hey, Jesus! You left the door open!

JAMES: What's the matter, Jesus? Were You born in a barn? (ANNA *starts laughing and nods emphatically.)* Oh yeah, I guess He was.

(They laugh again and return to their game. ANNA *stops in midjump.)*

JAMES: What did you stop for?

ANNA *(thinking):* James, do you think maybe sometimes we're a little too hard on Jesus?

JAMES: Of course not. I mean, look how miserable He's made things for me. I can't ever get away with anything because Mom and Dad know that He always tells the truth. If I try to fight with Him, He just gets nicer to me. He's so courteous, it makes me sick.

ANNA: Well, look at the bright side. At least we always get to ride in the front seat of the camel.

JAMES *(not amused):* Funny. But anyway, that's not good enough. As soon as I get older, I'm going to move out of this place for good.

ANNA *(like she has heard all this before):* I know, I know. But let's finish our game first. *(She throws her rock and jumps to the end.)* Yes! I did it! James, I won!

JAMES *(angrily throws down his rock):* I'm not playing any more. I hate this game! *(He storms away.)*

ANNA *(calling after him):* James . . . James, come back. I'll let you win! *(She gives up on him and exits to the opposite side of the stage.)*

NARRATOR (JAMES): And Jesus kept increasing in wisdom and stature, and in favor with God and men. And Jesus was going about in all Galilee, teaching in their synagogues and proclaiming the gospel of the Kingdom, and healing every kind of sickness among the people. And the news about Him went out into all Syria; and they brought to Him all who were ill, taken with various diseases and pains . . . and He healed them. And great multitudes followed Him from Galilee and Decapolis and Jerusalem and Judea and from beyond the Jordan. Then the chief priests and the elders of the people were gathered together in the court of the high priest, and they plotted together to seize Jesus by stealth, and kill Him. [Luke 2:52; Matthew 4:23-25; 26:3-4]

Scene 2

*(*ANNA *and* JAMES *are now adults. Scene opens with* JAMES *working in his carpentry shop.* ANNA *enters nearly in tears.)*

ANNA: James, you've got to come home. We need your help.

JAMES *(busy and annoyed):* Oh, Anna, what is it this time?

ANNA: Jesus is in trouble. We have to go get Him and bring Him home.

JAMES: Look, Anna, we tried that before, and it didn't work. He won't come.

ANNA: But they said they're going to kill Him. I don't know what to do.

JAMES: Go home, Anna. He's made some people mad, but He hasn't broken any laws. They aren't going to kill Him.

ANNA: You're right, but Mom is really worried this time. Won't you just . . .

JAMES: Anna, go home. Can't you see I'm busy? (ANNA *sighs and walks away.* JAMES *starts back to work. Then, he reluctantly reconsiders. He throws down his hammer and packs up a bag.)* I guess I'd better go. *(He exits.)*

NARRATOR (ANNA): They took Jesus, therefore, and He went out, bearing His own cross, to the place called the place of the skull, which is called, in Hebrew, Golgotha. And there they crucified Him. [John 19:17-18]

Scene 3

(ANNA *is sitting on the floor, dejected.* JAMES *enters carrying his bag.)*

JAMES *(solemnly):* Anna?

ANNA *(looking up):* Oh, James. We were too late. Can you believe they killed Him?

JAMES: I don't know what to believe anymore. Is Mom all right?

ANNA: She's so confused. She thought Jesus was going to be a great leader or something. I never thought that, but still, I can't believe they crucified Him.

JAMES *(angrily trying to explain it all away):* Well, He was always causing trouble. He had a lot of strange ideas, and He never could learn to keep His mouth shut in front of the Pharisees.

ANNA: But He never hurt anyone. They didn't have to kill Him.

JAMES: They didn't want to at first. He taught about loving one another and loving God. But He put a lot of people off when He said they had to be born again to get into heaven. And when He suggested that He *was* God—that's when He really got into trouble. You know, I think He really started to believe that. He just got carried away, that's all.

ANNA: You don't think there's any truth to it then?

JAMES: About what?

ANNA: About Jesus being the Messiah?

JAMES: How could I? Anna, He was our brother.

ANNA: I know, but He wasn't like us. That was obvious. There was something different about Him.

JAMES: He was different, all right. Do you remember when we were younger and the Romans would come and make us carry their things? Jesus would always carry them twice as far. And from what

I hear, He was that way all His life. When He was hanging on the Cross, He asked God to forgive the people that were crucifying Him because they didn't know what they were doing. He always gave back good when people gave Him evil. I'd call that different.

ANNA: You have to admit, He was sincere about everything He said or did. It wasn't just a game with Him—He really cared about people.

JAMES *(angrily):* Well, if He cared so much for them, then why did those same people have to kill Him?

ANNA *(looking up, earnestly searching):* Maybe that's just it. Maybe He *had* to die . . . for them.

JAMES *(confused):* What are you talking about?

ANNA *(still searching):* And for us.

JAMES: Wait a minute, Anna.

ANNA *(she turns quickly to face him):* I don't understand it all, but maybe dying was His plan all along. You remember how the prophet Isaiah wrote that the Messiah would be pierced for our transgressions?

JAMES: Well, whatever His plan was, it's all over now. He's dead.

ANNA *(back down to earth):* Yeah . . . I'm . . . I'm going to go see if I can find Mom.

(ANNA *exits.* JAMES *looks up to heaven and prays.)*

JAMES *(slow and confused):* O God, can any of this be true? Jesus was my oldest brother. I've watched Him grow up since I was a small boy. He grew to be such a great teacher. I always knew He was different. He seemed to be closer to You than to any of us. My sister, Anna, thinks that maybe He *had* to die. But, why? Could it really be possible that my brother was the Messiah? *(Looks down and shakes head)* But that doesn't make any sense. *(Looks up again)* If He was the Messiah, then He came to save us—to bring us life. But how could He bring us life when He's lying in a grave?

Scene 4

(ANNA *rushes in, excited.* JAMES *enters from the other side.)*

ANNA: James! James!

JAMES: What is it?

ANNA: I've just seen Mother. She's been to the tomb. He's alive. Jesus is alive!

JAMES *(doubtful):* Oh, come on. Did she see Him?

ANNA: Yes! and Mary Magdalene and other people saw Him too!

JAMES: Do you believe them?

ANNA *(sincerely):* Yes, I believe them. Don't you see it, James? He's not just our brother—He's the Son of God. I believe it . . . *(She looks sternly into her brother's eyes.)* I believe it.

JAMES *(confused):* I don't know, Anna. How could this be?

ANNA *(frustrated at his doubt):* James, He's done everything He said He would do. (JAMES *ponders a moment, then decisively grabs a few things and puts them in a bag.)* Where are you going?

JAMES *(turns and faces her):* I'm going to find Jesus.

(ANNA *watches as* JAMES *leaves, content. She pauses then follows him. She stops and faces the audience with a smile.)*

ANNA: We know that Christ died for our sins according to the Scriptures, and that He was buried, and that He was raised on the third day, and that He appeared to Peter, and then to the Twelve. After that He appeared to more than 500 brothers at one time. And then *(pause, then sweetly)* He appeared to James.

Nicodemus and Joseph

A Readers Theatre Sketch for Lent

by Cynthia S. Baker

Cast:

READERS 1, 2, 3, and 4
NICODEMUS
JOSEPH OF ARIMATHEA

Setting:

Minimal or no scenery is needed. Choir robes for readers. Suits and tie for NICODEMUS and JOSEPH.

Production note:

Readers theater uses the script as the only prop. Lines should be well rehearsed and memorized, even though the scripts will be used. For more information on readers theater, consult Lillenas' *RT: A Readers Theater Ministry.*

(Stage is dark. Cast quietly sings "Let Us Break Bread Together." Lights come up slowly as readers speak.)

READER 1: The night we call Maundy Thursday was Jesus' last night on earth.

READER 2: It was the climax of His ministry . . . a time of great significance . . . a time of strange contrasts.

READER 3: It began quietly enough, with a very familiar ceremony—the Passover Feast. Jesus placed high value on this last meal with His disciples; He had planned it carefully so that they would be undisturbed.

READER 4: And when the hour came, He sat at the table, and the apostles with Him. And He said to them, "I have earnestly desired to eat this Passover with you before I suffer."

READER 1: But Jesus added something new to the old ritual. Using the bread and wine, familiar items, He established a new practice for His disciples, that they might remember Him always. We call it Holy Communion.

READER 4: And as they were eating, He took bread, and blessed and broke it and gave it to them, and said, "Take; this is my body." And He took a cup, and when He had given thanks, He gave it to them, and they all drank of it. And He said to them, "This is my blood of the covenant, which is poured out for many."

READER 2: He gave them another important symbol when, after supper, He knelt on the floor and washed their feet—a task that was usually assigned to the lowliest of slaves.

READER 4: When He had washed their feet and resumed His place, He said to them, "Do you know what I have done to you? You call me Teacher and Lord, and so I am. If I then, your Lord and Teacher, have washed your feet, you ought also to wash one another's feet. For I have given you an example, that you also should do as I have done to you."

READER 3: Thursday night was also the time of the betrayal of Jesus into the hands of His enemies by one of His friends. He knew who His betrayer was. He was not caught off guard.

READER 4: Jesus answered, "It is he to whom I shall give this morsel when I have dipped it." So when He had dipped the morsel, He gave it to Judas. Then Satan entered into him. Jesus said to him, "What you are going to do, do quickly." Judas immediately went out; and it was night.

READER 1: Jesus knew also that His other friends would all desert Him, and that His beloved Peter would even swear He had never know Him.

READER 4: Peter said to Him, "Lord, I will lay down my life for you." Jesus answered, "Truly, truly I say to you, the cock will not crow until you have denied me three times."

READER 2: The sad and solemn Last Supper was followed by Jesus' agonizing prayer in the Garden of Gethsemane, while His disciples slept. It was the only time His Father God had ever said no to one of His prayers.

READER 4: "Father, if Thou art willing, remove this cup from me; nevertheless, not my will, but Thine be done."

READER 3: Then suddenly, the dark, sad peace of the garden was shattered by noisy shouts and the flare of torches. The moment had come. Jesus faced His arrest with calm and courage; but the disciples ran like rabbits.

READER 1: His trial by the hastily assembled high council of the Sanhedrin was viciously unjust, and the outcome was predictable. Jesus was not only convicted but also physically abused. When morning came, they led Him away to the Roman governor for sentencing.

READER 2: It's a sure thing, though, that not all the members of the Sanhedrin were summoned to Jesus' trial. Jesus had at least two secret friends who belonged to that body of high-ranking men. Their names were Nicodemus, who had once questioned Jesus privately by night; and Joseph, from Arimathea, who later was to provide the tomb in which Jesus' body was buried.

READER 3: We can only imagine what these two men must have felt . . . and thought . . . and said . . . after they discovered what had happened to Jesus.

(JOSEPH *comes to edge of stage and pounds on imaginary door.* NICODEMUS *crosses the stage and opens the door for* JOSEPH.)

NICODEMUS: Joseph, I'm glad you've come. Please close the door.

JOSEPH: What is all this, Nicodemus? It's five o'clock in the morning! Your messenger said it was urgent.

NICODEMUS: Joseph, the Sanhedrin met last night at the house of the high priest.

JOSEPH: Impossible! It's illegal to meet without notice. As members, we would have to have been called.

NICODEMUS: We were not called because they didn't want us there. They had Jesus of Nazareth arrested, and at the meeting, He was convicted of blasphemy!

JOSEPH: No! Nicodemus, there must be some mistake!

NICODEMUS: It's a mistake, all right. *(Bitterly)* The whole hideous, illegal mockery of a trial broke every legal precedent the Sanhedrin has ever established for seeing justice done. The hasty assembly and the verdict without due process were both illegal. No defense witnesses were called. Jesus was spit upon and beaten. You know the law as well as I do, Joseph! Even for the worst of offenders, none of those things would have been allowed!

JOSEPH: But Jesus is the Son of God! You know it, I know it—He really is the Messiah! Did He not defend himself? He could have called the wrath of heaven down upon them!

NICODEMUS: He could have . . . but He didn't. He didn't lift a finger.

JOSEPH: Didn't He even tell them who He was?

NICODEMUS: Yes, finally. When the high priest asked Him straight out, "Are you the Christ?" Jesus said, "I am; and you will see the Son of Man sitting at the right hand of power, and coming with the clouds of heaven."

JOSEPH: Well, that was plain enough.

NICODEMUS: And then the high priest tore his robe, and shouted, "Why do we still need witnesses? You have heard his blasphemy—what is your decision?" And all the members of the high council who were there fell over one another in their eagerness to condemn Him to death!

JOSEPH: Condemned to death-for claiming to be who He really is! I knew many of them were becoming dangerously hostile, but I really thought Jesus could take care of himself—He always had before. Nicodemus, they are fools—wicked, wicked fools!

NICODEMUS: You are right, but it is over and done. Even now, they are dragging Him before Governor Pilate because they want Him to be put to death.

JOSEPH: We must do something. What can we do?

NICODEMUS: What can we do? There's nothing to do. Who would listen to us, with the high priest and all the Temple authorities and the whole Sanhedrin combined against us? We don't even have time to get to Pilate first.

JOSEPH: At least we are together. We should go to Pilate's palace. If there is any chance we can do something, we must be there.

NICODEMUS: Yes, let us go. We must find out what is going to happen next.

JOSEPH: Surely, Jesus can take care of himself. Surely.

(Blackout.)

The Week That Was—and Is!

By Barbara Rowland

Cast:

NARRATOR
SPECTATOR
SKEPTIC
SOMETIMES FOLLOWER
SEEKER

Setting:

Stage props consist of stools or upturned boxes for sitting as needed by the actors. Costumes should be uniform, perhaps blouses and shirts in different colors and navy slacks.

Production note:

The cast can be either male or female or any combination. Use your imagination in designing a set. You may add appropriate musical numbers by choir or ensemble between scenes and at the end. Also, feel free to produce scenes independently of each other as part of a larger program.

Scene 1

(NARRATOR *enter moves to center stage as lights come up.)*

NARRATOR: This is the week that was—and is. This is that week in Jerusalem about 2,000 years ago when a man called Jesus of Nazareth was crucified, dead and buried, and on the third day arose from the dead.

This is the week in [your city] about 2,000 years later when a man called Jesus of Nazareth is crucified daily and yet rises again triumphantly in the hearts of humanity.

This is a true story seen through the eyes of persons who were there. And it is a true reflection of the ways of seeing Jesus Christ by persons who are here.

The time is then and now—and somewhere in between.

The place is [your town].

The characters are unrecorded witnesses of the week that was—and people you may recognize from the week that is.

(NARRATOR *has been down center stage. He or she quickly moves offstage as* SEEKER *and* SPECTATOR *enter from opposite sides and meet at center.)*

SPECTATOR: Did you come to watch the parade?

SEEKER: Parade! I wouldn't call a new King coming into the city a parade.

SPECTATOR: Oh, I like to watch anything! I heard He is riding a donkey! Friend of mine knows the man His follower's borrowed it from. Did you ever! A donkey! Isn't that a hoot?

SEEKER: But I've heard some say that Zachariah foretold that. His riding a donkey fulfills a prophecy that said . . . *(thinks)* oh, something about the king coming to Jerusalem riding on a donkey. Wonder if there is a chance He might really be the prophesied King?

SKEPTIC *(enters stage right on line and joins them):* Ha! I heard that. Surely you're not serious! A traveling preacher with a bunch of ragged followers—that He might be a King! No way. When the Messiah comes, if there ever is such a time, it will be with great glory. The sooner this Jesus is silenced, the better. He stirs up the people.

SPECTATOR: He really has caused a stir. But it's fun to have something interesting happening. Something to watch—something to talk about. I would never get involved, you know, but I love to observe and discuss it all with my friends.

SKEPTIC: You and your friends better be careful talking about Jesus. I don't think He'll last the week here in Jerusalem. The city is packed, and there's more chance for a demonstration or something to upset the religious leaders even more. They're wanting to see Him put away, and His followers may go with Him.

SOMETIMES FOLLOWER *(speaking as he arrives):* Absolutely. I'm just careful about letting people know I believe Him. See which way the wind blows, you know. But I've heard His teaching and seen His miracles. I believe He is who He claims to be.

SKEPTIC: Fools! You've been taken in by a lot of smooth talk. It's a ridiculous claim. I know that . . .

SPECTATOR: Listen. I hear shouting! Here they come. What a crowd of people with Him?

SEEKER: Look. The children are placing palm leaves in His path. How sweet! What a pretty picture. And there He is on the donkey!

SKEPTIC: More people than I thought there would be cheering Him. That bunch of men right around Him must be the disciples. Poor, ignorant fellahs. They'll be running away soon enough, mark my words.

(Actors follow procession with eyes as it passes in front of them from stage right to stage left and as Jesus dismounts and enters the Temple, which is down left offstage. Eyes and bodies turn and follow. Gaze is just above the heads of the audience.)

SOMETIMES FOLLOWER: Blessed is he who comes in the name of the Lord!

SKEPTIC: Someone might hear you.

SOMETIMES FOLLOWER: Oh, it's OK when everyone around me is for Him. I'm just careful when I'm with other groups, that's all.

SEEKER *(hasn't been listening to the above exchange):* His eyes—they look right through you. He looked at me . . .

SPECTATOR: Isn't this exciting? I love a crowd. I almost feel like getting involved and shouting, "Yea, Jesus!"

SOMETIMES FOLLOWER: He is getting off the donkey at the Temple and walking up the steps. They're going into the Gentile Court.

SEEKER *(sits, pensive):* I think it would be good to have someone to believe in. There must be more to life than being born, working, reproducing, and dying. What's our purpose?

SKEPTIC: What do you mean—purpose? That's all there is to it. You make the most of your time and that's that. Don't get hung up on religion and meaning. You can't believe that stuff. It doesn't hold up in the real world where people suffer.

SPECTATOR *(cheerfully):* But, it's fun to observe. I'm having a great time. But I don't let it get to me. I don't bother with it. I just watch it.

SOMETIMES FOLLOWER: Belief in Jesus Christ as the Son of God gives us a relationship with God. Don't you want that?

(SPECTATOR *shrugs.)*

SEEKER: I'm not sure I understand. I don't know how to . . .

SPECTATOR: Listen to the yelling. What's happening at the Temple? People are rushing out.

SKEPTIC: The money changers and the sacrifice sellers are leaving in a hurry. What on earth is going on? With the huge crowds in town, this should be one of their best days.

SEEKER: Could Jesus . . . I mean, would He oppose them? Would He have the nerve to . . . ?

SOMETIMES FOLLOWER: Of course He would! That's it! You know how people are cheated in there. He probably told them to get out.

SPECTATOR: Oh, goody! I'm so glad I came to see this. Ooooh, who's that man hurrying this way with the bird cage?

NARRATOR *(playing dove merchant, hurries in pantomiming holding a large bird cage):* Whew! *(Sets down cage)* Let me stop and catch my breath. *(Sits)*

SKEPTIC: What happened over there?

NARRATOR: This preacher-guy came in. You've heard of Him? Jesus? *(He looks around at the others who nod.)* Well, He got really mad 'cause we charge so much for our sacrifices. Just started turning over tables and running us out. I scrambled in the dirt to get my spilled coins, grabbed my birds, and here I am. And this was going to be a really busy day. He has no right. Somebody will stop Him!

SOMETIMES FOLLOWER: I've heard Him say His Father's house has become a den of thieves. Good for Him! He did some housecleaning!

SKEPTIC: His Father! Ha.

SEEKER: He certainly isn't afraid of much. I'd like to believe that strongly in something.

SOMETIMES FOLLOWER: He may need some support. I'm going over there.

(SOMETIMES FOLLOWER *rushes offstage.)*

SKEPTIC: I don't care what they do to Him. None of my affair. Have enough problems of my own without caring what happens to someone who claims to be the Son of God.

NARRATOR *(angrily stands):* I want to see Him silenced. He has caused enough trouble. Some nerve telling me how to run my business. Sure, I charge 15 times what they do outside the gates, but my doves pass inspection and those bought outside don't. Even after I pay the inspector, I make good. It's all in a day's work.

SEEKER *(stands, sarcastic):* Sure it is. Like cheating on your income tax or on a test . . . like padding your expense account or taking long lunch hours on your employer's time. All in a day's work. Everybody does it. *(Looks toward Temple)* Maybe He knows a higher way.

SPECTATOR: Well, I don't care what happens, just so I get to watch it. I've got to run. Wait till my friends hear about this. See you later.

(SPECTATOR *exits, others watch her leave. Blackout.)*

Scene 2

(NARRATOR *enters, moves to center stage as lights come up.)*

NARRATOR: The Christ who was—and is—sometimes followed, sought, observed, raged against, scorned . . . takes a day of rest in the middle of the week at the home of a friend in nearby Bethany. While Jesus, His host, and the other guests are at dinner on an open terrace, an unusual thing occurs. The reaction to it differs as it does today.

(NARRATOR *exits stage left as* SPECTATOR *and* SEEKER *enter from center aisle.)*

SPECTATOR: I can see well from here. *(Kneels down center)* Now I can see Jesus at the table and His followers all around. This hillside outside the terrace is a perfect place to be. I can watch what happens.

SEEKER: You're always watching. Don't you ever *do* anything?

SPECTATOR *(laughs):* Not unless I have to. I don't want to get involved, you know. I'm what the psychologists call passive. You see, since I grew up with television, I can easily switch my brain into neutral, and I don't have to think or react—just watch and be entertained. But you're a fine one to talk. Why did you want to come out here with me?

SEEKER: Seems I can't stay away from Jesus this week. I've never spoken to Him, but whenever I can, I follow Him. I heard He had come to Bethany today, so when I got off work I wanted to come here. And I met you on the way. People are camped everywhere between here and Jerusalem. Someone said there are 2½ million people here for Passover.

SPECTATOR: Wouldn't doubt it.

(Both continue to look at terrace, SPECTATOR *with obvious overinterest.)*

SKEPTIC *(entering from stage left):* Hello, you two. What's going on? I visited a friend here today, and I'm headed home. What are you doing?

SEEKER: Hi. We're just "Jesus watching" again.

SKEPTIC: New pastime, huh? Like I told you Sunday, He won't last long . . . and since then He has really upset the powers that be. He'll be put to rest soon, I'll wager.

SPECTATOR: Look! That woman has come in and is approaching Jesus with that bottle. Looks like alabaster . . . I wonder what . . . ?

SEEKER: Looks expensive. What could be in it?

(All watch intently.)

SPECTATOR *(astonished):* She has pulled out the stopper . . . and she's pouring something on His head!

SKEPTIC: What a dumb thing to do. That's bound to be expensive perfume. Shameful waste.

SEEKER: She's anointing Jesus!

SOMETIMES FOLLOWER *(hears last line as he enters from stage right):* Anointing Him? She must recognize who He is. The talk is that Jesus may be arrested this week—and tried. Perhaps she is anointing Him for burial in case the worst happens. She's giving Him her very best, it seems. I should like to do that if I had an alabaster jar of perfume.

SKEPTIC: Even for a believer, that's ridiculous. Extravagant gesture, if you ask me . . .

SPECTATOR: That's a real touching picture. I wish all my friends could watch this with me.

SEEKER *(to* SOMETIMES FOLLOWER*)*: But couldn't you make better use of it? Like sell the perfume and help the poor?

SOMETIMES FOLLOWER: Jesus teaches to care for the poor. You're right about that. But He has said, "The poor you have with you always." I think Jesus honors giving your best to Him.

SEEKER *(stands):* Your best for the Son of God. Of course. We wear our best clothes to worship. Why not the best we have for our King. I can understand that now. And that's an answer for us when we complain about the cost of things—like better windows—or new hymn books. Our best for our Lord!

SPECTATOR: That woman certainly gave her best. I wouldn't do it, but I'm glad I saw it!

(Blackout.)

Scene 3

(NARRATOR *enters and moves to center stage as lights come up.)*

NARRATOR: The week that was—and is—progresses to Thursday evening. It is the time for the Passover feast, a sacred meal commemorating the Jewish deliverance from slavery in Egypt. It is the time for a plot to arrest Jesus, the man who has aroused anger in the religious leaders by His claims to be the Messiah.

(NARRATOR *leaves stage.* SEEKER *and* SKEPTIC *enter, walking together stage right. They turn and go down center.)*

SKEPTIC: So two men followed you home and asked your father to use this upper room for the Passover?

SEEKER: Yes. Father was glad to let them use it, since they would prepare their own feast and didn't ask us to do it. The men asked to use it for their teacher. I didn't know at first it was for Jesus. Father asked me to find what they needed, so I spent the afternoon with them. I learned so much about Jesus, the man they follow.

SKEPTIC: So you helped that rabble-rouser and His fanatical followers get ready for the Passover feast. Why are you so excited? Why did you want me to come here?

SEEKER: I want you to look. *(Both go down center)* See, right here through this crack. Can you see them? OK. The third one from the left and the one next to him are the two who followed me. That's Jesus there.

SKEPTIC: I recognize Him. Well, why did you want me to see this. It's just a bunch of men around a Passover table. Just like what's happening all over town.

SEEKER: Because, I thought you might see . . . might feel . . . well, might hear something that would make you . . .

SKEPTIC *(angered):* What are you trying to say?

SEEKER: This afternoon, being around those men and hearing them talk about Jesus, His miracles and His teachings, well, it made me think. The coming of the Messiah is the core of my faith. Why should He not come now?

SKEPTIC: Now, don't you jump on this fanatical bandwagon too! Mark my words, this bandwagon is about to crash against the strong wall of organized religion. You better not be on it.

SEEKER: But what if we reject the true Son of God? He could give meaning and purpose to these lives of ours.

SKEPTIC: Huh? I've got enough purpose trying to make a living. Don't think I could handle any more. I must be gone. Don't do anything foolish.

(SEEKER *has been peering through the crack on last line. As* SKEPTIC *starts away,* SEEKER *calls out to him.)*

SEEKER: Wait! Jesus said one of them will betray Him! And a man is leaving the room. I'll go with you. I don't want to be seen.

(Lights black out very briefly and come back on SOMETIMES FOLLOWER *and* NARRATOR *as the high priest enters.)*

SOMETIMES FOLLOWER: Since we talked yesterday, I've had second thoughts about our agreement. (SPECTATOR *enters quietly and "hides" as she realizes that something juicy is about to happen.)* Thirty pieces of silver to arrange for you to arrest Jesus . . . well, I've been a follower for quite a while. Perhaps I . . .

NARRATOR: Now, we've been over all of that. You want what's best for your people and your country. Why, if Jesus is who He claims to be, the members of the Sanhedrin will recognize it, and He'll not be harmed. We just can't arrest Him for questioning in the midst of a crowd. There might be a riot. You let us know when and where. Then the matter is out of your hands. You'll not be responsible for what happens. Surely you don't put yourself on the spiritual level of the Sanhedrin, do you?

SOMETIMES FOLLOWER *(hastily):* Oh, no! Of course not. It's just that I . . . oh well, I would like the silver, and it's not such a bad thing to point Him out to you—just show you where He is, right? You're going to get Him anyway. Someone else will do it if I don't.

NARRATOR: That's right! And you must look out for yourself. Now, here's the bag of coins. You lead us to Him tonight.

(NARRATOR *exits.* SPECTATOR *comes up behind* SOMETIMES FOLLOWER.)

SPECTATOR: I heard that! (SOMETIMES FOLLOWER *jumps and turns.)* You didn't know I was watching. Oh, don't worry. I don't care. I won't tell. But would you tell me something? You say you're a follower, and yet you will sell Him out. Why?

SOMETIMES FOLLOWER *(angrily):* It's no big deal. Followers sell out Jesus all the time. And for less than 30 pieces of silver. Why, He is sold out for television, popularity, sex, or even mowing the grass. At least I got silver. *(Shakes bag in front of* SPECTATOR*'s face)*

(Another quick blackout with lights coming up as SEEKER *and* SPECTATOR *move toward center stage.)*

SPECTATOR *(shivering):* Why did we come out here? What's so great about Gethsemane. It's cold tonight.

SEEKER: You like to watch, don't you? Well, watch with me. After the Passover Supper, Jesus and His disciples walked up the Mount of Olives to the Garden of Gethsemane for prayer. I wanted to come and figured you would, too, since I have a feeling something may happen.

SPECTATOR: OK, OK. But you know I don't want to get involved. Just observe. I'm a viewer, not a participant. So, don't try to get me into anything.

SEEKER: I'm not. See . . . there are the disciples up ahead.

SPECTATOR: Looks like they're just sitting around. Most of them are asleep. That's silly to come all the way out here and then sleep.

SEEKER: Hush. They're probably waiting for Jesus. He said He was coming to pray. There He is under that huge olive tree! See, in the that patch of moonlight?

SPECTATOR: Now I do. Let's get closer. *(Creeps a step closer)*

SEEKER *(pulling* SPECTATOR *back):* No! I feel . . . embarrassed. Like we probably shouldn't be looking. He seems to be in such agony. We're invading His privacy. Let's step back . . . behind this tree.

(They move behind a "tree.")

SPECTATOR: Listen. I hear people coming. Oh, look! Temple guards and lots of others. There's that Follower we talked to at the parade last Sunday.

SEEKER: Let's stay out of the way. I think Jesus is about to be arrested!

SPECTATOR: The Follower kissed Jesus.

SEEKER: Look, that one took a swipe at the guard! He cut his ear off!

(Both draw back in disgust/fear. Then lean forward in unison. Raise eyebrows and drop jaws.)

SPECTATOR: Jesus put the ear back on!

SEEKER: Look! The guards are putting Him in cuffs. We better get out of here.

SPECTATOR: No! I'm staying! All of the disciples are running away. Where are you going? (SEEKER *dashes away.)* Oh! He's running past the guards. I can't believe it! He shook away from the guard. But the guard got his outer clothes. Well, there goes Jesus. Hauled away like a common criminal. Guess you can't blame followers for running away. The cost of being a disciple may be more than they're willing to pay. *(Shrugs)* Glad that doesn't affect those of us who observe while things happen.

(Blackout.)

Scene 4

(NARRATOR *enter moves to center stage as lights come up.)*

NARRATOR: The Spectator, the Seeker, the Skeptic, and the Sometimes Follower are among us—or in us—today. The Spectator, the Seeker, the Skeptic, and the Sometimes Follower were present the Friday that Jesus was crucified. After a night and early morning of farcical trials, He was cruelly beaten and made to carry His cross to Calvary where He was hung between to thieves. He hangs there, dying.

(NARRATOR *exits.* SEEKER *enters slowly and sits on stool down center. Appears lost in thought.* SPECTATOR *enters and takes seat on stool opposite him.)*

SPECTATOR: I thought I'd find you here on the roof. Isn't the weather pleasant for early spring?

SEEKER *(forcing himself to speak):* Yes, it is. *(Glances about)* Usually we have more wind now. The flowers are opening up with such a grand show of color. See the garden below. *(Nods to area offstage)*

SPECTATOR: It's beautiful! Makes me ready to get new spring clothes.

SKEPTIC *(enters as waiter):* What'll you have?

SPECTATOR *(brightly):* I think I'll have coffee.

SEEKER: Same here.

SPECTATOR *(to* SKEPTIC*)*: I'll need lots of cream and sugar. You have such a lovely view of the garden up here.

SKEPTIC: Messes up our view a bit today, seeing those crosses on the hill there. But it'll be over and they'll be down soon enough. Guess that preacher fellow wishes He'd kept His mouth shut in Jerusalem this week.

(SEEKER *and* SPECTATOR *look at each other.)*

SPECTATOR: Well, I don't know about that. But it has been some show to watch. Hasn't been so much excitement and confusion during Passover Week ever.

(SKEPTIC *nods and moves upstage.)*

SEEKER *(has been staring at cross since it was mentioned except for glance at* SPECTATOR*)*: Did you watch Him carry His cross up the hill this morning?

SPECTATOR: Oh, I did, and it was awful! His body was bleeding, and He kept falling. I could barely watch.

SEEKER: I went up the hill too. I wish that I had the nerve to offer to carry the cross for Him. *(Pause as* SKEPTIC *reenters with coffees.)* If He is who He claims to be, what will happen because He was put to death?

SKEPTIC *(places coffee in front of guests):* He couldn't be the Son of God. Why would He hang on a cross? Besides, if a loving God who sent His Son for us really existed, there wouldn't be all the trouble in the world—all the sickness and hunger and crime—the threat of nuclear war. So, don't go getting worked up over an agitator dying out there today. *(Brightly)* Anything else?

SEEKER: Cream, please. Thanks. But His disciple told me that day of Passover that it's because of our own free will and the evil we choose that we have those things. He said that Jesus is the Messiah and that through Him we can have a relationship with God.

SPECTATOR: I don't understand all that. (SOMETIMES FOLLOWER *enters.)* Hey, that man coming in—isn't he the follower we saw at Gethsemane with Jesus?

SEEKER *(calls to* SOMETIMES FOLLOWER): Come over and join us.

SOMETIMES FOLLOWER *(agitated):* Well, if you're sure it's all right.

SPECTATOR: Want some coffee? (SOMETIMES FOLLOWER *nods and* SKEPTIC *goes for a cup.)* We were just talking of the morning's events. You knew Jesus, didn't you?

SOMETIMES FOLLOWER *(hastily looks around):* Well, I . . . I used to be . . . are you working with the Sanhedrin?

SPECTATOR *(laughs):* Do we look like religious higher-ups? No way. I'm just a spectator.

SEEKER: And I'm just . . . well, perhaps you could say I'm a seeker. Seems to me there should be more to life than what to eat and what to wear. I wonder if this man being put to death out there had some answers to what it's all about, and I think . . .

SKEPTIC *(enters and interrupts):* I know what it's all about. It's about earning a living, paying taxes, and dying. That's what it's all about. *(Leaves)*

SOMETIMES FOLLOWER: I thought He had some answers. *(Looks at crosses)* Now I don't know. There He hangs, dying on a cross—He who claimed to be the Son of God. But some say that all that has happened so far fulfills prophecy, and He won't stay dead but will rise on the third day.

SEEKER *(harshly):* If that is so, how ironic that we should sip coffee and discuss weather while we kill the Son of God.

(All stare at crosses.)

SPECTATOR: We watch.

SOMETIMES FOLLOWER: And we wait.

SEEKER: But that's the way it always is. We eat and drink and make conversation while the world dies.

(Loud rumble. Startled looks. Lights begin to dim as rumble increases and then stops. Lights continue to dim out on following lines.)

SKEPTIC *(entering):* What's happening? The earth shakes.

SEEKER: The sun is disappearing!

SOMETIMES FOLLOWER *(overwhelmed at the significance of it all):* What have I done?

SPECTATOR: It's turning dark. But, it's noon!

SEEKER: We've killed the Son of God!

(Blackout.)

Scene 5

(NARRATOR *enters and moves to center stage as lights come up.)*

NARRATOR: The day began as any other first day of the week. Families awoke, dressed, ate the morning meal, and prepared for work or school. It didn't seem like a day that would change history—and the lives of all people who accepted by faith what happened on that spring morning.

(NARRATOR *exits.* SEEKER, SKEPTIC, *and* SPECTATOR *rush onstage and stop center as* SEEKER *points straight ahead.)*

SEEKER: See! There's the empty tomb, just like I told you! It's true! Jesus is alive! He arose from the dead!

SKEPTIC: Likely the body was stolen by the disciples, and they're spreading the story that He rose from the dead.

SEEKER: No! They didn't expect it! Besides, the tomb was guarded by Roman soldiers.

SPECTATOR: How do you know all this?

SEEKER *(acting out his story):* Let me explain. Early this morning, I decided to walk out here. On the way, I met two Roman soldiers running toward the city. I wondered about it, but I didn't know they were the ones guarding the tomb. Well, I got near here and stopped by those shrubs there. Right away, I saw there were no guards and the stone was rolled aside.

About that time, one of the women who was at the Cross came hurrying up that path carrying spices. She was about . . . here before she looked at the tomb. She saw the stone was moved, and she stopped short. Then she cautiously crept up to the entrance.

Suddenly, a man stepped out and spoke. He looked like a vision, but when he spoke, I could hear. He said, "Why do you look for the living among the dead? Jesus is not here. He is risen."

She stepped inside the tomb to look, and the man disappeared. She came out weeping, and another man was there. He asked her why she cried, and she said the body of her Lord was gone. Then He said, "Mary," and she looked at Him and fell on her knees and cried, "Master!" It was Jesus! He's alive.

(Pause)

SKEPTIC: If He did come alive again . . . could He be the Son of God?

SPECTATOR: We've watched this drama unfold all week. I can't just observe anymore. I must act on what I've witnessed . . .

SEEKER: And what we have witnessed is the fulfillment of God's plan. Now I have purpose in my life—to live it for God, who sent His Son to die for my sins. Praise the Lord!

(All three stand together full front. SOMETIMES FOLLOWER *joins them.)*

SPECTATOR: There are always . . . spectators.

SKEPTIC: There are always . . . skeptics.

SEEKER: There are always . . . seekers.

SOMETIMES FOLLOWER: There are always . . . sometimes followers.

ALL: For all of us, Christ died . . . and arose!

(NARRATOR *enters and joins them.)*

NARRATOR: And that's the way it was. And that's the way it is. Christ died and arose and lives today.

ALL: Praise the Lord!

(Blackout.)